The Great North Road Through Babworth Parish

by

Joan Board

ISBN 978-0-946404-62-9

2013

The Nottinghamshire Heritage Series

THE JOHN MERRILL FOUNDATION

Dedication

To Sarah and Mary

Acknowledgements

I would like to thank all those patient people who have opened their doors to me: Mr. and Mrs. Holder, Mr. and Mrs. Morrell, Mr. and Mrs. R. Howard and Mr. and Mrs. MacMaster. In addition Mrs. Elliott, Mrs. Wright, Mrs. Cowley and Mr. Bayes have been most helpful in supplying otherwise inaccessible information. Without the support and encouragement of many friends at Babworth Church this work would not have been possible.

CONTENTS

Introduction   4

Jockey House   . 7

A Sense of Place: Morton Grange   12

Little Morton and The Roman Legacy   15

Rushey Cottages and Scrooby   18

The Old Rectory at Babworth   · 24

Babworth Hall   33

Field Names   40

INTRODUCTION

A Landranger map, Sheet 120, shows the thin, yellow line of a road 'generally less than four metres wide' appearing to start at the edge of Gamston Airfield. For a couple of miles this road pushes up north through the ancient Hundred of Bassetlaw, becoming little more than a track in some places, in others a pot-holed lane.

Yet this almost forgotten stretch was the Old North Road until the coming of turnpike roads in the eighteenth century caused it to be re-routed through the market town of Retford. The by-passed road lies between the North Road and its twentieth century replacement, the A1.

Because of that eighteenth century re-routing this section of the Old North Road has remained undeveloped and able to yield not only the hard facts of its past but also tales of colourful romance.

Long before it was a road there was a track here on a dry ridge, striding the undrained marshes. In the second half of the twentieth century evidence of the existence of pre-historic settlements on this part of the road has been recorded. In 1980 Dr. Derrick Riley published 'Early Landscape from the Air', the result of six years work mapping crop marks on the Sherwood sandstones of North Nottinghamshire. These showed a previously unsuspected system of land division, drainage and habitation at the side of this part of the Old North Road.

As a result of the aerial photography some preliminary archaeological excavations were carried out in 1981 at Dunston's Clump (named after a nearby wood) where artefacts from at least the first century B.C. were discovered. A decade earlier an axe head had been turned up in an old drainage ditch on adjacent land and was dated as 1850 BC by the Sheffield Museum. This suggests that when Abraham, Isaac and Jacob were farming the Holy Land, men were

THE OLD NORTH ROAD THROUGH BABWORTH PARISH

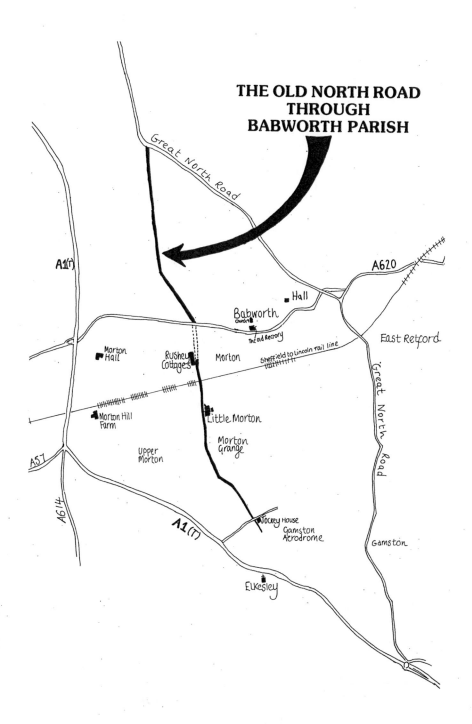

farming here and walking a track which, centuries later, would be known as the Old North Road.

What skirmishes and departures there were in Roman times are unrecorded but may be guessed at from the caches of coins dug up in the vicinity over the years. Such archaeological finds argue a substantial and continuous presence hereabouts.

Along this route King Richard I chased a deer to the death beyond the Nottinghamshire boundary. This is the road that stretches between Sherwood Forest and Barnesdale, both places contenders for the home of Robin Hood. King John travelled along here from his hunting lodge in nearby Clipstone. Aware of the dangers of travelling these lonely, wooded roads, he issued a decree in 1285 that all trees and bushes for two hundred feet either side of such roads be removed in order to hinder highwaymen.

This old road has presence and purpose, moving directly on its journey between London and Scotland through one of the loveliest spots in the land. In contrast the re-routed turnpike merited G. K. Chesterton's description:

> 'The rolling English drunkard made the rolling English road'

In places on this section summer hedges are wreathed in honeysuckle and briar rose, as though time has forgotten them. A ten foot high wild rose hedge echoes Walter de la Mare's sentiments:

> 'Oh no man knows
> Through what wild centuries
> Roves back the rose.'

The rich, royal, famous and infamous travelled this road — Princess Margaret Tudor, Cardinal Wolsey, Henry VIII, John Evelyn and Dick Turpin among others whose stories are remembered in the historic houses that remain here.

A beautifully crafted gypsy caravan, a frequent visitor, with its line of washing, grazing horse and pan boiling on the wayside fire adds to the air of time standing still.

6

Jockey House

Standing as it has done for centuries, Jockey House is now most attractively restored as a house and adjacent cottage that retain its former identity as a coaching inn. At its side the Old North Road peters out in a grass track halting at the airfield fence.

Surprisingly, Jockey House is not listed yet it must have some claim to be among the oldest of the county's buildings.

A previous owner, who made extensive renovations, left notes of what was found for the benefit of the occupants. He

An early eighteenth century sketch of Jockey House as it looked in Dick Turpin's time

mentions daub and wattle walls dating from the fourteenth century, arched brick windows indicating sixteenth century work as well as headers and stretchers in the brickwork, wire cut bricks and pegged beams. Other signs of early building methods were found upstairs where floors, constructed of lime and pebble, were laid over bulrushes.

In the living room the original fireplace remains: through its wide chimney the sky is amply visible. So are ledges, as deep as steps. One ledge in particular is much deeper than the others. The significance of this became clear in the nineteen sixties when the roof was replaced. Slung underneath it was a large box-like construction, a priest hole, which at a later date served Dick Turpin when the law was after him.

A long oral tradition links Dick Turpin with houses along the Old North Road but with Jockey House in particular. As late as Edwardian times wagonettes brought tourists down this lane to see where the infamous highwayman hid.

In summer this is a tranquil spot with crops and water sprinklers stretching towards Rufford Abbey and Clumber Park. Ancient Sherwood is on the horizon. An occasional green bus rattles past the door to cross the A1 making for Mansfield or Nottingham.

In past centuries Jockey House seems to have been a daunting place with a gibbet on the crossroads outside the door. An extant eighteenth century sketch shows what a lonely place it was. As if to emphasise its remoteness the Jockey Stone, which still stands, records that it is '142½ miles from London.'

As an inn it had an astonishing past featuring guests as desperate and even more mysterious than Dick Turpin.

The Jockey Stone giving the distance to London and to Worksop Manor and informing travellers that the key for unlocking the road could be had at Jockey Inn. It is in position on the sketch.

One was a young girl who stayed at Jockey Inn more than three hundred years ago. Her sad story has been handed down by people who were sufficiently concerned about the injustice done to her to pass the story on.

Eventually the brief account of her murder was written in block capitals on a page torn from an exercise book in the early years of this century and passed on to the owners with the deeds. The story refers to the murder of Lady Caroline 'in the sixteen hundreds,' predating another murder in 1721 which attracted national publicity. In the intervening years improved communications — especially the spread of newspapers — had ensured that news travelled both farther and faster.

Lady Caroline's story is intriguingly brief. Travelling by coach she arrived late at night and took a room at Jockey Inn. The next morning she was missing. The account tells that the innkeeper was in a bad mood because he suspected that she had left early to avoid paying her bill. Much later in the day he went to the cellar to draw beer and noticed something dumped behind the barrels.

It was the body of Lady Caroline. The crime appears to have gone undetected.

What is now Jockey House was the actual inn, the present cottage the living quarters of the innkeeper. There were no more than three rooms for guests so even if those were occupied on the night of the murder there were few suspects.

An amazing aspect of the crime is that Lady Caroline's body was found in the cellar under the living quarters of the innkeeper. That was a long way to carry a body through the archway that still separates the two dwellings and past the well which was the only source of water and must have been in fairly frequent use.

Jockey House has kept its secret: the mystery will never be solved. In its refurbished state with smooth lawns, neat hedges, fresh paint and flower-filled tubs, Jockey House looks the unlikeliest scene of such a crime.

Yet not only Lady Caroline met a violent death there but John Baragh's life was also cut short.

On 24th June 1721 a company of guards travelling south down the Old North Road stopped at the Jockey Inn for refreshment. John Baragh had been there before the guards came in.

The Captain, Midford Hendry, was a sociable man who liked company and talking. He knew his own mind and spoke it; he had no time for anyone who disagreed with him. When the Captain began discussing politics John Baragh disagreed with him. To emphasise the truth of his argument Captain Midford Hendry drew his sword. Possibly he intended only to put a country bumpkin in his place. If he had been sober he would perhaps have had greater control over his actions.

Elkesley Churchyard with John Baragh's gravestone recording the murder at Jockey Inn 1721

The fact is he ran John Baragh through in a most professional way and the civilian died immediately. Four days later he was buried in Elkesley churchyard where the leaning, crumbling gravestone reads, 'murdered 24.6.1721 aged 29 years.'

There is an interesting footnote to this story, involving a strange coincidence.

Unlike the murder of Lady Caroline which appears not to be recorded but has survived through an oral tradition, the Baragh murder in 1721 was reported in a London newspaper.

A painter and decorator told the RETFORD TIMES on 10th October 1902 — a hundred and eighty years after the murder — that was when he was an apprentice forty years before, he was helping to renew mirror and picture frames at Elkesley vicarage. These are his words referring to that occasion in about 1860:

> 'We ran out of paint and sent up by mail to London for a supply of gold for colouring. The firm in London sent the colouring back wrapped in an old newspaper. This newspaper, a London one, contained an account of the inquest on John Baragh who was murdered at Jockey House by Captain Midford Hendry.'

So, by a coincidence, a hundred and forty years after the murder, a man in the vicarage attached to the churchyard where the victim is buried reads his story. Forty years after reading it he passes it on to a local newspaper and almost a century later it is recorded on microfilm in the local history library.

There is something about the name of this prepossessing house that is slightly disturbing. It carries some connotation that accords more with its history than with its present appearance. For, from medieval times 'to jockey' meant to deceive, to cheat.

There is the mysterious and somewhat sinister incident of the title, Jockey of Norfolk, being used of Sir John Howard, the first of that name to become Duke of Norfolk. He was a loyal supporter of King Richard III, fighting with him at the Battle of Bosworth where both he and the King were killed. The night before the battle Sir John returned to his tent to find this strange warning:

> 'Jockey of Norfolk be not too bold
> For Dickon, thy Master, is bought and sold.'

Retrospectively that smacks more of dirty tricks than prophecy.

A Sense of Place: Morton Grange

Morton Grange, a hundred yards farther up the Old North Road from Jockey House, was set up as a sheep farm in 1170 by the monks of Rufford Abbey. Since that time the land has been in continuous cultivation.

Journeys made by monks must have been hazardous. There were wolves in Sherwood Forest; indeed three centuries later Sir Robert Plumpton was still granted land by the crown for his office of keeping the wolves down. Nearby the monks would be able to see the palace King Henry II built. That was a fabulous place, the Royal Centre Parcs of its time, with chantry, vivarium (fish pond), mill, farm and wine stocks. Medieval monarchs hunted there, held summit meetings and outdoor parliaments under the Parliament Oak. The ruins in the tiny village of Clipstone are known today as King John's Palace, named after King Henry II's son.

Morton Grange looks out over open land which has seen fewer buildings erected in the intervening centuries than most other counties of Britain.

When the monks arrived with their four hundred sheep the soil was poor: it was dry and sandy with gorse and bracken. As more land was reclaimed from ancient forest the difficulties of farming it became evident. What the struggle cost in earlier times is not known but since the time of the Enclosure Act in the eighteenth century, records show its upkeep has been a constant battle.

To Morton Grange has been added Upper Morton Grange, in total 2,145 acres of land in cultivation on either side of the Old North Road. There are no sheep now but a variety of crops — Aegean blue linseed, wheat, barley, sugar beet, peas, potatoes and carrots. It takes sixteen tractors and two combines to harvest them. In the season lorries pull as much as a hundred tons of sugar beet a day up the road.

Not only is Morton Grange fully mechanised but a computer

print-out gives at a glance the crop, variety and field name. Indeed there is something anachronistic in seeing the poetic names, Badgers' Eighteen Acre, Four Oaks, Donkey Field, Cherry Breck, Front Grindle and Jockey Leys issuing from a computer. Nevertheless it is satisfying to see such names as Mercia — for this land was in that ancient kingdom when the Venerable Bede was writing his history. Mercia Winter wheat, Pipkin Winter barley and Blenheim Summer barley remind us that agricultural methods change but man's needs are the same as when royalty was hunting deer and Robin Hood was poaching it on this very land.

In this dry, infertile area water has always been there, underground, sometimes as near the surface as fifteen feet. But it was not until the late twentieth century when technology made it accessible through sprinklers that the land could become so productive. Modern irrigation techniques have solved an age old problem.

However it does seem worth recalling one farmer who lived at Morton Grange from 1917 until 1959. Before irrigation techniques were available Joseph Camm appreciated the nature of the land at Morton Grange and made it pay. He built up the fertility of the soil so that he never had land lying without a saleable crop. Thus early potatoes were lifted in June and on the same day the land was worked and Savoy cabbages planted. When they were taken up the following January winter wheat was set. He kept bullocks for manure, brought in sheep in thousands to consume crop residues and 'add their golden hoof to soil fertility.'

During the hungry forties of the Second World War and its aftermath he was much sought after by farming experts for his expertise in producing vegetables during a time of grave national shortage.

It is interesting to discover that he used a penny exercise book in which to keep his crop notes. He was a man of his time reluctant to change horses for tractors: horses produced offspring and also kept the land fertile.

Yet however much modern technology has improved agricultural yield the place retains its ancient identity.

Everywhere in the two thousand acres are reminders of its history. For instance, the large, well-defined fields with their trimmed hedges are the same fields, of the same size, that were enclosed by the Duke of Newcastle under the Enclosure Acts between 1750 and 1780. There are forty miles of hedges altogether on the Morton Grange farms, despite the fashion in the second half of the twentieth century for destroying them.

The unique historic feature that identifies Morton Grange is its earthen cellars. Speculation suggests they were constructed and used by the monks to connect their living quarters with their chapel, located by the side of the Old North Road in Chapel Field. Some archaeologists consider the cellars may pre-date the monks: certainly Mortun, the settlement on the marsh, is mentioned in the Domesday Book.

In the twentieth century two uses for the cellars have been recorded: initially as wine cellars, then as an Air Raid Shelter when the Sheffield blitz was at its height. Their origin is still uncertain but given the resurgence of interest in local history and their proximity to this ancient road, their mystery may yet be solved.

The old Morton Grange, of which one photograph remains, fell into disrepair when used to store grain in the early sixties. The house looked interesting and individual, too good for a warehouse. Its successor, built in 1975, is worthy of the ancient name and long tradition of the place.

Little Morton and the Roman Legacy

Along the Old North Road key houses take their name from the Domesday term, Mortun, a settlement on the marsh. Apart from Morton Grange and Upper Morton mentioned previously there are Morton Hill Farm and Morton Hall estate as well as Little Morton.

Little Morton is the archetypal English Manor House. Standing sideways to the road in a seventeenth century style it could serve as the settling for some Sherlock Holmes or Miss Marple story. There is an air of mystery and seclusion about it, even on the sunniest day.

Little Morton is a misnomer in every way for the house is large and imposing with a conglomeration of outbuildings of some antiquity. Surprisingly it remained an unlisted building until the mid nineteen eighties. For many years the property belonged to the Dukes of Newcastle, as did many of the houses in the area. It is difficult to establish its age as it has obviously been extended over the years. A fire at Clumber House in Clumber Park destroyed many records belonging to the Newcastle estate, including details of Little Morton. Nevertheless the title of Lord of the Manor of Little Morton survived and was sold in the early nineteen eighties. The present owners did not bid for it although the family has farmed here since 1888.

Certainly rear parts of the present house with daub and wattle walls, low ceilings, beams, uneven floors and tongue and groove doors with snecks, are very different from rooms at the front of the house. These are graciously proportioned with large, unusual windows and impressive marble fireplaces. The main staircase is iron and gives on to a mezzanine floor in between the first and second storeys and continues up to a third level.

Structurally similar to the house the present owner's grandfather came to over a century ago, the inside has easily adapted to every modern convenience from microwave to jacuzzi. Elegant, lived-in and, above all, interesting, the house combines past and present. In the spacious, modernised kitchen, the original bacon hooks — eight were stipulated in the bill of sale — remain. On one of them hangs a well worn, initialled bird-scarer not dissimilar to an an old football rattle. Over the fireplace there is an asymmetrical dosing horn, another sign of the way ancient and modern live together.

On the wall in the passage outside the kitchen there is a framed tapestry of Queen Victoria as a girl riding a pony and attended by her favourite dog. The picture was embroidered by the present owner's great great grandmother when she was thirteen years old. As she was born in 1830 the embroidery would have been done only four or five years after Queen Victoria came to the throne.

Among other unusual relics of the owner's long tenure is an Enclosure Map of the fields, as taken in by the eighteenth century acts. The boundaries of the property are drawn in a curve on fine, white cotton. Within the curved boundaries the fields have ruler straight edges. Each field has its area recorded in indelible ink. At first glance these appear to be dates e.g. 18.8.68, 31.3.08. Actually they are measurements in acres, rods and poles. An accompanying parchment document gives a key to the measurements, supplying in addition the names of the fields. Thus what is commonly called Holly Bush Close about the farm is recorded on the map as Hollin Bush Close showing how usage changes the pronunciation of words.

Perhaps the most intriguing thing about this document is that it refers throughout to the Old North Road as the York Road. Thus fields bordering it are Middle York Road Close, Upper York Road Close etc., perhaps indicating an even more ancient name for the Old North Road. It is possible that the name is a legacy of Roman days. York, their Eboracum, was a goal of the Romans before people could or did travel to Scotland.

The Romans did travel this road and they did stay at what is now called Little Morton. The land yielded ample evidence of that in 1989. An occasional artefact had been thrown up from time to time but that year two men with metal detectors turned up a large cache of Roman coins. Altogether three thousand three hundred coins were retrieved. The owner of Little Morton thinks their retrieval was made possible by the fact that he had reached the subsoil when ploughing the land the previous year.

On being examined at the museum, the coins were dated at aboutA.D. 250 and were found to include thirty or so counterfeits: it appears that human nature has not changed much over the centuries.

Further excavation by a local history group yielded another three hundred coins and chards of their container. This major discovery poses a number of questions about the owner of such an enormous number of coins at a time when coins were not common. It suggests the possibility of there being a villa where Little Morton now stands.

Such a discovery on land bordering the Old North Road is by no means unique. A stone tablet set up in 1807 on the Morton Hall estate commemorates the finding of 62 copper and 29 silver Roman coins.

On other neighbouring land a farmer in the nineteen seventies unearthed an axe-head in a drain which the museum dated as 1800 BC thus confirming possible farming hereabouts since Biblical times.

Rushey Cottages and Scrooby

Leaving Little Morton the Old North Road crosses the Sheffield to Lincoln rail line. It then runs down through a copse to an intriguing red brick building with pointed gables, red roofs and tall chimneys rising from the long, low line of a medieval inn. Now three cottages, this building must be one of the oldest in North Nottinghamshire.

Known as Rushey Inn, it was already well established when King Henry VII's daughter, Princess Margaret Tudor, stayed there in July 1503.

Rushey Cottages and the Old North Road leading up to Scrooby. The chimney pots in the form of beer barrels remain from the days when the building was an inn

It is a larger, more imposing structure than Jockey House, and was regarded as suitable to accommodate a King's daughter who was on her way to marry another King, therefore it was chosen rather than the Jockey. Recent aerial photographs indicate the Rushey Inn used to be the centre of a cluster of buildings. This would have made the inn a suitable choice so that the princess' considerable entourage could be accommodated near to her. Unfortunately only the inn remains today.

Although the royal visit happened so long ago the story is recorded in great detail giving ample insight into the customs of the time.

Princess Margaret Tudor was born in 1489, the eldest ·daughter of King Henry VII and sister of the future King Henry VIII. She ·was born only four years after her father, Henry Tudor, had fought and killed King Richard III at Bosworth, thus bringing to an end the long Wars of the Roses. The princess, who was fourteen years old, was escorted as far as Northampton by her father in a long and lavish royal procession. Then the King returned to London leaving Princess Margaret to travel with great ceremony through Nottinghamshire, escorted by nobles and soldiers. After staying at Tuxford she spent two more nights in the county.

Contemporary accounts show how Tudor times earned the appellation, 'Merry England.' The bells of Elkesley Church, a stone's throw from the old road and now standing on the A1, rang out all day. The villagers from miles around were given a public holiday to greet the Princess.

Several hundred people walked the two miles from Retford to Rushey Inn to pay their respects on the morning after her overnight stay. Led by the Reverend Thomas Gunthorp, rector of Babworth parish, four other clergymen, two bailiffs and twelve aldermen, they set off betimes because they were there and back by noon. From the bedroom window where Princess Margaret slept it would have been possible for her to watch the procession most of its way along the winding, dusty lanes. The third storey room above, with its dormer window and commanding view, would have been an ideal look-out for a security guard.

The account that has come down of the Princess' stay states that she was 'mightilye well pleased' with her reception. So memorable was her stay at Rushey Inn that even as late as 1920 when the property was being sold it was referred to in the estate agent's brochure as Margaret Tudor House.

The Retford procession on that July morning in 1503 did not go empty-handed. They took with them:

4 bottles of Malmsey	2s.	8d	(13p)
1 lagon (sic) of red wine		8d	(3p)
4 tubs of ale	6s.	11d	(35p)

In addition to this they 'payed two mynstrelles two shillings and fourpence!'

This brought the total cost to 12s. 11d. (64p). However the aldermen paid 'each of them for himself 3d.' Thus the charge on the commonalty was 9s. 11d. (50p).

Again the Princess said she was 'Mightilye well pleased with the honour done to her.' After leaving their gifts the Retford procession 'retired in the same order in which it had proceeded' and the royal party left the little inn which has remained so proud of the memory of that royal day. Although the Rushey has been converted into three cottages since the time of Princess Margaret Tudor's visit, there have been few structural alterations and none of the refurbishment that Jockey House has undergone. A wooden frame around the window in the bedroom where the Princess slept supports the ceiling. When this same ceiling was patched in the early eighties, it disclosed the ancient rushes that had been used in its initial construction.

Some of the decayed ceiling beams in the first floor bedrooms have been added to with ship's timber. The use of such material for renovation is a reminder of the long period when the nearby River Trent was navigable and the town of Bawtry, where the Princess was handed over to the keeping of the High Sheriff of Yorkshire the next day, was an inland port.

An interesting feature of the first floor at Rushey Cottage is yet another concealed room. There is an eight foot length of wall between two bedrooms unaccounted for by the size of those rooms. It is impossible to say now whether that concealed room was there in 1503 as, by their nature, such places were kept secret. Its existence is acknowledged from the eighteenth century because from that time it was referred to locally as Dick Turpin's room. As with Jockey House and Little Morton the concealed room may have been a priest hole. Three existing examples of such places of concealment in such close proximity must be very unusual.

Interesting outbuildings from coaching days remain at the rear of Rushey Cottages. The old forge with its patched and crumbling brickwork retains its wide chimney breast and, until the nineteen eighties, its original chimney remained.

When Princess Margaret Tudor's procession resumed its journey to Barnby Moor it was met and accompanied by 'great numbers of people.' Considering how rural and sparsely populated this part of the country was, and still is, those people must have walked considerable distances to be there.

Her next overnight stop was at Scrooby, the last village on the Old North Road in Nottinghamshire, where the Archbishop of York had his Palace. As soon as this came into view the cavalcade halted. Johannes and his mynstrelles were again called on and continued to play all the way to the entrance gate of the Palace.

At that point the arrival of the future Queen of Scotland was announced by trumpeters and the drawbridge raised. Once the royal party had passed inside the drawbridge was closed for the night.

The visit must have contrasted strangely with the stay at Rushey. The moat of Scrooby Palace contained six acres, bounded on its northern side by the River Ryton. It was the hunting seat of Archbishop Savage, 1501-1508, at the time of Princess Margaret Tudor's visit. Aptly named, the Archbishop was the kind of clergyman that Shakespeare was shortly to put into his plays. He was a courtier, a formidable politician and, as an afterthought, a cleric. Probably the hastily closed drawbridge was more for his protection than that of the Princess as the previous night's stay at Rushey Inn seems not to have incurred such security precautions.

Certainly the Palace at Scrooby entertained many famous visitors, including the Princess' brother, a boy at this time, but destined to become King Henry VIII. As King, he sent his Antiquarian to make an inventory of the Palace.

This officer, John Leland, has left a valuable description of Scrooby Palace in the early sixteenth century:

'A great manor palace standing within a moat and builded into courts whereof the first is very ample and all builded of timber save the front of the hall that is of brick to which you ascend by steps of stone.'

Early in the morning after her overnight stay the trumpeter sounded the rally for the royal party who 'proceeded with musik and banneres' to the county boundary and thence up the Old North Road to Edinburgh where her future husband, King James IV of Scotland, met her in early August.

Unlike Rushey Inn, the great Palace at Scrooby soon fell into decay. By 1675 the building had completely disappeared. Thoroton, writing at that date, says:

'Here within living memory stood a very fair palace, a far greter house than Southwell and it hath a fair park belonging to it . . .'

Although few traces remain of its moat and boundaries traditions persist. One such recalls that Cardinal Wolsey, who stayed at Scrooby Palace for more than a month when he was out of favour with King Henry VIII, planted a mulberry tree in the grounds. It was on the occasion when he heard the prophecy of Mother Shipton that he would see York but never enter it. The Cardinal laughed and promised to see the hag burned. Nevertheless it proved true. Within sight of York he was recalled by the King and died on the way back to London.

As for Princess Margaret Tudor, life treated her harshly: ten years after this royal journey her husband, King James IV of Scotland, was killed at the Battle of Flodden fighting against her brother, King Henry VIII of England. At twenty four she was a widow with a young child, King James V.

An ironic footnote to the visit is provided by the Jockey Stone. It still stands near to where the fourteen year old Princess 'was mightilye well pleased with the honour done to her,' pointing the way to Worksop Manor 7 miles away. This was one of the places where Princess Margaret Tudor's granddaughter, Mary, Queen of Scots, was held captive as a young widow. After fleeing Scotland she became the prisoner of Queen Elizabeth I who gave her into the keeping of the Earl of Shrewsbury at Sheffield Castle. In Spring when the castle was being cleaned the royal prisoner was taken to Worksop Manor for safe keeping

A further irony was Princess Margaret Tudor's stay at Scrooby. The Master of the Queen's Post at Scrooby was to be William Brewster who, besides being one of the original Pilgrim Fathers, was in the employ of a man who carried out the death sentence on Mary, Queen of Scots. It is strange that in such a small, country place so far from London there should be two such connections.

The Old Rectory at Babworth

Leaving Rushey cottages the Old North Road becomes a cart track as it must have looked before the turnpike roads were made when stage coaches averaged four or five miles per hour.

Standing two hundred yards to the east and commanding a good view of this stretch of road is the Old Rectory. An impressive white house set among mature trees, it could be part of a film set, especially in a spacious Nottinghamshire sunset. On this same spot a parson's house has stood for seven centuries, probably longer.

The Old Rectory can be viewed from the lane leading up to Babworth Church. Now called Haygarth House it is owned by Pump Maintenance, a private company that has carefully restored and preserved the character of both house and grounds. Presently it functions as a Training Centre for the

The Old Rectory, Babworth, 'many gabled, many chimneyed.' The second window from the left on the top floor is the haunted room

24

Company and also as a hotel and conference centre to accommodate national and international — especially American — tourists.

As it stands, whatever the season, its intrinsic appeal is immediate. Surrounded by an ancient copse, it looks out on a mass of snowdrops from the end of January until the Mothering Sunday primroses replace them. These, in turn, are followed by a tide of bluebells. Sharing its seclusion with the adjacent churchyard it is a rare, untrammelled part of England retaining the tranquillity of Gray's Elegy:

'Far from the madding crowd's ignoble strife
Their sober wishes never learned to stray;
Along the cool, sequestered vale of life
They kept the noiseless tenor of their way.'

The loudest sounds here are the call of the cuckoo, the ceaseless morse of wood pigeons and the song of the blackbird and thrush. In winter the robin's song is as sharp and clear as the clock's chime.

Arthur Mee found the Old Rectory delightful — 'many chimneyed, many gabled.' Taking tea on the lawns in front of the house under the ancient beech and cedar with the roses in bloom is a pleasurable experience. All kinds of recollections of 'dear, dead days' come to mind especially Rupert Brooke's picture of forever England with 'the church clock at ten to three' and 'honey still for tea.' Inside the house there is a photograph of the Wilberforce family taking tea on the lawn in 1917. The Reverend Wilberforce, the last rector to live here, was a descendant of both the slave reformer and Soapy Sam, the Bishop of Oxford. When Soapy Sam was asked why he had this nickname he replied, 'Because I'm often in hot water and always come out with clean hands.'

The whole ethos of the house provides a link in a living chain that secures us to the past in a positive way that record offices, reference libraries, microfilm, microfiche and precious books cannot. Even so, the hard-earned information gleaned from these valuable sources opens up the magic and mystery of houses that might otherwise be taken at face value only.

For instance, the Old Rectory in its many forms over the centuries has housed some amazing clergymen.

One of the ministers, William de Grendon, was actually murdered. Considering his record it was surprising it did not happen sooner.

> 'Confessed misconduct with Ellen, daughter of John de Ryparis, ordered to pay her £20. 29 Nov. 1309.'

> 'Accused, with others, 11 Sept 1312, of abducting Eliz, wife of Henry de Camville, at Arrow Warws.'

> 'Owed £1,000 to Edmund de Shireford, 7 Oct. 1327.'

> 'Owed £100 to Thos de Saundby 3 Feb 1332.'

> 'Imprisoned 1330 owing to trespass against Ralph de Crophill and others.'

> 'Killed at Babworth. Thos de Grendon indicted but pardoned.'

This is an amazing record for any priest and all the more so considering that parsons at that time took a vow of celibacy.

Nor was he the only rector who met a suspicious end. Thomas Heald, whose official brief account of his work in the parish remains, dated September 10th 1743, states:

> 'I do reside Personally upon my Cure, and in the Parsonage House. I have no curate. I do intend, while it shall please God, to enable me, to perform the whole Duty myself.'

Thomas Heald supplies valuable information about the population of the parish:

> 'There are twenty five families. Two are of the Romish Perswasion. There is no licens'd, nor any Meeting House. There is no Publick nor any Charity School.'

He ends his account by saying:

> 'I have not met with any uncommon Difficulties in the Discharge of my Duty, I have no objection in Relation to the Canons and Discipline of the Church, nor any complaint against Ecclesiastical Officers.'

Nevertheless Thomas Heald, of Babworth Rectory, drowned on the sixteenth of June 1759 while bathing in St. John's Well in a neighbouring village. This raises the question of whether parsons usually bathed in wells or whether there were 'Difficulties in the Discharge of his Duty' that his parishioners were more aware of than he. It is reminiscent of how men from the nearby Isle of Axholme dealt with the Dutch who came to drain the land — by throwing them in the water and using long poles to hold their heads under.

The many gracious rooms of this lovely listed building have seen many worthy men in addition to a few rogues.

There was Thomas Gunthorp, rector from 1494/5 to 1535/6. Not only did he lead the procession that welcomed Princess Margaret Tudor at Rushey Inn in 1503 but at his own cost 'erected a school house at Retford in 1518.' This was Retford Grammar School which still continues to educate children from the area as it has done for almost five centuries. After Thomas Gunthorp's time several of the parsons who lived at Babworth Rectory taught at Retford Grammar School.

Of course there were some parsons who held the living of Babworth in the eighteenth century who never set foot in either church or rectory. Guy Fairfax was a case in point: presumably he obtained the Babworth living because he married the patron's niece. Another priest in the same century held fourteen other livings in addition to Babworth. That is reminiscent of the poet, George Crabbe, who returning to his living after a ten year absence, was astonished to find the congregation converted to Methodism.

From 1838 to 1895 the Reverend Bridgeman Simpson was the rector. He rebuilt the house since when it has undergone no structural alterations. On coming to the rectory the Reverend Bridgeman Simpson, who during the previous year had married the daughter of the fifth Earl Fitzwilliam, was required by his father-in-law to bring the house up to a standard suitable for his daughter's station. During the fifty seven years that he was parson at Babworth he refurbished the church and the rectory. He performed both tasks so well that no further restoration was needed until the second half of the twentieth century.

The improvements to the Old Rectory were on such a

grandiose scale that by 1935 no parson could afford to live there and a new rectory was built by the side of the Old North Road.

The spacious rooms and winding passages of the Old Rectory have seen, over the centuries, most of the prototypes that appear in literature such as Fielding's Parson Trulliber, idle, ignorant and self-willed; Jane Austen's sycophantic snob, Collins, must have made more than one appearance among those eighteenth century absentee parsons and surely Trollope's gallery included some of Babworth's rectors.

The most notable occupant of the Old Rectory was Richard Clyfton who came to the house in 1586 and stayed until he was deprived of his living in 1605. He was obliged to leave Babworth Church and Rectory because the views he held conflicted with the views of the Church of England of his time. Calling himself a Separatist, as distinct from a Puritan who wished to purge the church of its Romish practices from within, he wanted to draw apart from these evils. He was not the first rector at Babworth who wished to change church doctrine and practice. In 1581 the Reverend Robert Lylly appeared to have Puritan leanings as he refused to wear a surplice.

The difference between these two rectors seems to have been their degree of conviction. The Reverend Richard Clyfton held more positive views which he preached at discussion groups in the rectory after church services. In the Old Rectory he was joined by two disciples, William Bradford, an orphan from Austerfield, who walked nine miles every Sunday to hear him preach and William Brewster, mentioned in the Rushey Inn chapter in connection with the execution of Mary, Queen of Scots.

If it is apposite to call Columbus the Father of America, then it is equally appropriate to call Richard Clyfton the Father of Americans. Although this deprived rector, exiled in Amsterdam where he died in 1616, never reached America, the two Founding Fathers who sailed on the Mayflower in 1620 were fired by his ideas.

William Bradford, who spent time in the Old Rectory learning from the older and more scholarly Richard Clyfton, became Governor and Historian of the Pilgrim Fathers. In this latter capacity he left one of the few comments ever made about this most famous occupant of the Old Rectory:

'a grave and reverend preacher who by his fervour and diligence had done much good and under God had been the means of the conversion of many.'

As Professor Arber, a well-known American writer on the Separatists says:

'the Pilgrim movement originated in the church and rectory of Babworth in Nottinghamshire.'

The nineteen years that the Clyfton family spent in this old Rectory must have been harrowing, especially for the wife who gave birth to six children here. Three died in infancy and were buried in the churchyard. Only one of the six survived his father.

In the recent refurbishment of the Old Rectory the story of the Pilgrim Fathers has been kept alive. Conference, Dining and other Communal rooms each bear the name of those who left this house for America. As well as the people already mentioned, the women and children who were made homeless and exiles by their menfolk's beliefs are also remembered. The strange names, often based on Biblical texts, illustrate the dogma of parents who baptised children as Love, Wrestling, Fear, Peregrine, Oceanus.

Another name commemorated in the Old Rectory is that of the Reverend Edmund Jessup, the first rector not to live there. By the time he took up the living in 1950 the new rectory was well established. Yet it was he, in the English tradition of the parson who is writer and local historian, who uncovered the Pilgrim Father connection with Babworth Old Rectory and did so much to foster ties with America.

During the Second World War the Old Rectory functioned as the Number 5 Area Headquarters of the Air Ministry Directorate of Works. The house was leased to the Ministry in 1940 when the latter was relocated from Louth to Lincolnshire.

A staff of one hundred used the rooms as office accommodation. To provide further accommodation an annexe was built and the stables and outbuildings converted.

Additional buildings were constructed to serve as garages and a canteen. The Air Ministry made few internal alterations.

Keeping the building warm was an onerous task. Apart from a central heating system serving the ground and first floors, all the other rooms had small, cast iron fireplaces with open fires that had to be cleaned out and lit every morning and maintained regularly throughout the day. Carrying coal up to the attics and keeping the old-fashioned open range working in the kitchen took up most of a handyman's day.

During the Second World War the grounds and kitchen gardens were well maintained by a full time gardener. There was a good supply of fresh vegetables for the canteen. Peaches, tomatoes and cucumbers were grown in the greenhouse and the surplus was sold to staff.

Ministry employees could use the tennis courts in summer and life must have had some of the grace experienced by the rectory families in the nineteenth and early twentieth centuries. In 1960 the Air Ministry relinquished its lease on the Old Rectory.

With all the chances and changes the Old Rectory has seen and the varied human conditions it has witnessed it would be strange if it did not have some traces of the past. Sadness has been known to linger round battlefields, churchyards and ancient stones.

Several people swear that there is a presence in the Old Rectory and its surroundings. A policeman's dog, although impeccably trained, refuses to go up the lane where it narrows and where the trees overhang between the Old Rectory and the churchyard. There is a rider whose horse shies at the same spot. There are Pump Maintenance men who cannot stay in a certain room on the top floor, although it is a pleasant room with a beautiful view. This has caused letters to be exchanged and visits to be made by members of the Wilberforce family.

It seemed that when their father went to the Old Rectory in 1914 there had been some kind of scandal. The Library reveals nothing; the oldest inhabitants are tight-lipped. But, by chance, a lorry driver from the parish was given a pile of newspaper cuttings when he was in a village ten miles away. A yellowing cutting with the headlines: VILLAGE SENSATION. RECTOR AND LADY MISSING. PAINFUL SURPRISE. tells how the Reverend Curtis caught a Liverpool bound train early one morning while his wife and twenty year old daughter were on holiday in Scotland. He is described as about fifty years old, an eloquent preacher with a kindly disposition. It also reveals but doesn't name the 'Lady of Quality' from the same parish who is missing, having caught a train from a village station the same morning.

Further research reveals that the 'Lady of Quality' was the daughter of the previous rector of Babworth and, until her marriage to a gentleman of the parish, lived in the Old Rectory. An additional sadness that the parish registers reveal about this affair is that the deserted husband had been married before, his bride dying on honeymoon three days after the wedding.

Shortly after the Reverend Curtis left, his deserted wife committed suicide in a bathroom on the top floor of the house. This was still a bathroom when the Wilberforce family moved into the Old Rectory. It is now the bedroom that the administrator of Pump Maintenance has difficulty in filling.

The Reverend Wilberforce was known to hold liberal views concerning the burial of persons who committed suicide in consecrated land. In fact, in a corner of the churchyard where burials were taking place in 1914, there is an unusual stone without a name or any writing to distinguish it.

The significance of this tragedy was overshadowed by the outbreak of the First World War. In any case a scandal was suppressed. Nevertheless people who knew nothing of these events claim to have seen a ghost, a 'Dark Lady.' A woman recently going to Midnight Communion on Christmas Eve watched a dark figure walk from the churchyard through the car park to the little wicket gate of the Old Rectory. The churchgoer noticed the dress was old-fashioned and wondered at a lady going alone down the path to a building that was closed. It didn't occur to her at the time that what she saw was a ghost.

The church cleaner, now retired says, 'Oh yes, the Dark Lady's always about at Lily of the Valley time. I've often heard her sigh.'

A lady who worked as a cleaner in the Old Rectory while the Air Ministry occupied it, says there was always someone walking about the attics, opening and closing doors, although she never saw anything herself.

The Dark Lady is an unsurprising feature in this intriguing place. She is another link in a long chain that connects so very many people to the Old Rectory.

The wicket gate between Churchyard and Old Rectory where the Dark Lady walks

Babworth Hall

There has been a big house where Babworth Hall stands since before the Conquest. Its existence was recorded in the Domesday Book when the owner was Roger de Busli who received the house and land in payment for his services to William the Conqueror in 1066.

After the Conquest land values depreciated considerably, this estate being worth only ten shillings (50p) as against forty shillings (200p) fifty years before. A reason for its depreciation was inefficient farming and the absence of the French landlord who also owned half the county of Nottinghamshire. As Roger de Busli died without an heir, the ownership of the land reverted to the Crown who rented it out for half a knight's fee i.e. three shillings and fourpence (17p) annually.

By the thirteenth century the de Grendons owned the Hall and estate. This was the same family, one of whom held the church living and was murdered by a relative as recounted in the chapter on the Old Rectory.

Since the sixteenth century the owners of Babworth Hall have held the advowson (the right of choosing the rector of the church).

During the seventeenth century the Elwes family added a wing to the house; about 1715 John Simpson made further additions and alterations to transform the Hall into a Queen Anne house. Early in the nineteenth century the Hall and Park underwent considerable improvements. The famous landscape artist, Humphrey Repton, was engaged to landscape the grounds.

In order to do this, land in the immediate vicinity of the house was cleared of seven cottages that were rented to families working on the estate, and a windmill. The main Retford to Worksop road, the present A620, was diverted, by order of Quarter Sessions 1814, resulting in the seclusion of both Hall and Church.

Repton's celebrated Red Book shows what a master of advertising he was. His sketch of the Hall and estate, before the landscaping, pictures a bleak terrain reminiscent of King Lear's heath, where the owners are unable to stand upright in the gale. After the proposed landscaping the picture shows an incredible climate change where people sit and saunter in sub-tropical conditions.

Babworth Hall was the kind of country house where Jane Austen's characters went to stay when summer made London intolerably unfashionable. When Humphrey Repton was earning fame and fortune fashionable people found the country acceptable to live in, even for part of the year, only when it had undergone civilising improvements. It was the era of the stately Parks (as opposed to the medieval Deer Parks), ha-has, summer houses and, in extreme cases custom built ruins.

As Kipling was to express it later in the century,

'Our England is a garden
that is full of stately views,
Of borders, beds and shrubberies
and lawns and avenues,
With statues on the terraces
and peacocks strutting by . . . "

Humphrey Repton's most significant achievement at Babworth Hall was the creation of a nine and a half acre lake, a much-loved, much-described feature of the estate for a century and a half. It incorporated two small islands connected by a wooden bridge, a boat-house, a summer house and was flanked by banks of rhododendrons. As Arthur Mee described it in 'The King's England:'

'Swans glide by the wayside on the lovely winding
lake, from which fine parkland rolls up to the
creepered hall . . . encircled by mighty horse
chestnuts, sycamore, yews, cedars and beeches . . .
A singularly charming spot it is . . . though the stir
of Retford is only a mile away.'

Old Retford newspapers carry nostalgic accounts of skating by moonlight in Christmas Card winters when the Lake froze.

Anglers, too, have left excellent records of fishing from the Lake including pike up to twenty eight pounds, eels up to four pounds and perch up to one pound. In 1929 it was recorded that a salmon was caught making its way up the stream to the Lake. Every August Bank Holiday Monday Retford Angling Association held its annual match there when Sir Albert Whitaker presented a gold medal to the fisherman with the heaviest catch.

There seem to be several reasons why Repton's Lake dried up. One is that North Nottinghamshire is one of the driest regions in the country. Another is that in 1952 Retford Corporation made a borehole six hundred yards to the south of the Lake: this was soon pumping a million gallons of water a day from underground supplies in the bunter sandstone. The third and chief reason is that a stream that Repton dammed to make the Lake dried up. This stream, fed by a spring near Jockey House, was diverted when the Air Ministry took over the airfield adjacent to Jockey House in World War II.

Now, in place of the Lake, there is a modern, outdoor swimming pool set among Repton's tall cedars, hollies and yews. Flower-fringed and sun-warmed, the pool is approached along a woodland path and down steep steps. There is no doubt that the landscaping is still impressive almost two centuries later. From the air the lay-out of lawns, gardens and trees which are by now majestic, is elegant and dignified.

The Estate Diary, completed by Sir Albert Whitaker in 1929, gives some idea of the duties as well as the pleasures of a country landowner. In the Foreword it says:

'This was written so that many facts, which might otherwise become forgotten, should be placed on record.'

It does indeed record flora, fauna, field names and oral traditions it would be impossible to trace from other sources from the time Sir Albert's father leased Babworth Hall from Colonel Denison in 1898:

'Along the bottom of Far Whiskers small plantations of Alder, Black Italian Poplar, Ash and Poplar were made in 1898.'

And the same year:

> 'In order to improve the shooting three plantations of
> spruce and larch were made, Forest Young Trees
> and Broom Wood in 1890 and the New Planting
> Young Trees in 1900 while in order to increase the
> shooting my father rented the shooting rights of
> some 620 acres on both sides of Common Lane.'

At the same time Sir Albert Whitaker started to keep the
Estate Diary in 1896, hedges that were set after the Enclosure
Acts of 1780 and their consequent effects on farming methods
in the parish are things that old men remembered from their
fathers' conversations. The same oak and thorn hedges still
denote fields that were then enclosed.

From 1896 to 1914 the rich and famous of English Society
were entertained at Babworth Hall. Extant photographs show
royalty among house guests that enjoyed the vast acres of
shooting rights. The Prince of Wales, shortly to become King
George V, was a frequent visitor to the house with its
electricity 'and engine,' bathrooms, racquet courts, cricket
pitch, Lake and boathouse.

In the nineteen eighties the diary that the valet kept of this
period was published, with photographs of both English and
Norwegian royalty and the journey that the household made
in 1910 to a Norwegian royal wedding.

At the outbreak of the First World War the Whitaker family
of Babworth Hall took an active part. Sir Albert joined up with
his valet (who died of trench fever in the Autumn of 1914 and
was brought back to Babworth to be given a military funeral
and burial in the churchyard) and many of the estate workers.
The memorial in the church tells of Babworth men who failed
to return: it is a formidable list for such a tiny parish, with three
brothers dying in some families.

The Hall was a hospital between 1915 and 1919; six
hundred men were treated as patients, thirty being
accommodated at any one time.

During the summers of 1915 and 1916 the 62nd (West
Riding) Division and the 63rd (Northumbrian) Division were

Pen & Ink Sketch of **BABWORTH CHURCH**, Nr. Retford by Riflen. **Ramsden Farrar** (3505) **2/7th W.Y.R.**

A memento of the First World War. Rifleman Ramsden drew this sketch in 1915 while training on the Babworth Hall estate before going to the Western Front

encamped in Babworth Park and Bowman Hill. These troops carried out trench digging in the Whisker Hills area of the estate. This was in keeping with the tradition established by the previous owner, Colonel Denison, who trained soldiers here during the Boer War.

At the same time as British soldiers were carrying out these exercises a hundred yards away German prisoners of war were housed in a camp alongside the Old North Road. Most of the prisoners worked on building an aerodrome there; a few were boarded out with farmers in the parish.

Ironically enough, these war preparations were centred adjacent to Broom Wood — where the present A620 from Retford to Worksop intersects the Old North Road. Tradition has it that the Danes fought a battle here. Certainly ninth century Danelaw has left names alongside the road including Daneshill, a mile to the east of Babworth Park, as well as the above-mentioned Bowman Hill.

Babworth Hall estate leased land to provide an aerodrome to train the Royal Flying Corps in the First World War. In the early thirties the airfield and equipment was sold. Within a few years the site was opened as an army camp and served the same function until the nineteen sixties when it became a prison.

Babworth Hall as it was when Humphrey Repton landscaped the estate

Little Morton. View from the field where the cache of Roman coins was discovered. See page 12.

There was an early experiment in flight in 1910 on the Babworth Hall estate. An aeroplane hangared near the stackyard made attempts to glide from Bowman Hill 'but the machine crashed the only time it left the ground.' It was from these early, dedicated attempts that flight has achieved the sophistication it enjoys today.

Certainly the First World War sadly affected the Hall and estate. One result was the increase in burials and the need for the estate to provide land for a churchyard extension by 1915. The first person to be buried in the new part was a German prisoner of war.

By the second half of the twentieth century Babworth Hall was in need of repair and reorganisation. As was the case with the Old Rectory, the Hall had become too big for its lifestyle. Accordingly its size was reduced by a third. This historic house and site had undergone yet another change without suffering a loss of antiquity.

All kinds of things go through one's mind when faced by such a building. So many people have had a hand in this; so many people have left their mark here.

One thinks of those who lived in caves and scratched pictures on the walls; one thinks of a child coming home with that first precious picture from school and the person who, so many thousand years ago, scratched a horse's head on a bone in a cave at Creswell.

Whether you leave something on a bone or in stone the message seems to be the same: 'I was alive. This is what it was like.'

Field Names

On either side of the Old North Road 'the landscape is plotted and pieced, fold, fallow and plough,' a living echo of Gerard Manley Hopkins' description of nature's 'Pied Beauty.' In order that this land may afford pleasure to the eye it has to be worked and maintained. To do this efficiently the farmer needs working names or a grid reference number for his fields. This latter system is used more in countries where agricultural land was developed later than in England. Naming fields, rather than numbering them, is by far the more interesting alternative.

The names given to fields over many centuries both recorded and unrecorded tell much about the type of countryside, its geography and climate, the people's lives, their eating habits, their worship, fears, even their brand of humour.

Each of the fields and woods accompanying the Old North Road at this point has a name that tells a story. Sometimes oral traditions give an interpretation at variance with the official dictionaries of place names.

An example of this is the name of the parish of Babworth. Officially it is interpreted as Babba's place, as in Babbacombe, half a country away. Apart from the fact that this latter name implies a genitive, there is no record of anyone named Babba.

Moreover, an unsigned article in a mid-nineteenth century Retford newspaper gives the origin of Babworth as Pab-wyr, the early British for bulrush. This seems feasible as the terrain was marshy and used to flood both during and after Vermuyden's drainage work a few miles to the north-east. In addition the name occurs in Rushey Inn and Rushey Sidings; rushes were used in the construction of early ceilings.

The interpretation of the name of the River Idle is similarly dual. 'Idel' in old English meant empty or vacant, gradually taking on the meaning of useless or lazy. As it is a meandering river in this part it would seem to take its name from that. People whose forbears have lived here for generations say that it means 'the shining river.' This accords more with the modern German meaning of 'edel' as precious or glorious.

Philip Howard writing in 'The Times,' August 1989, suggested that some names originated in pre-literate times and survived into literate ages. They could have been spread by mass migrations, perhaps for survival during intemperate periods.

This area, lying a few miles south-east of the limestone ridge on which Creswell stands, shared a similar Ice Age lifestyle. Then herds of reindeer, wild horse and ox, woolly rhinoceros, mammoth and the hyenas that preyed on them, migrated via the land bridge to Holland before the ice melted to form the North Sea.

Indeed, fishermen off Dogger Bank have trawled up moorlog containing the bones of such animals, as well as plant remains, identical to those found in the caves at Creswell. Geoffrey Grigson, in his 'Country Writings,' gives examples of such finds. Dr. Jenkins, a Ranger at Creswell Crags, has archaeological evidence to support the theory that in the Ice Age there was land travel and communication more extensive than after Britain became an island. As the history of this terrain predates records it is likely that some of the names in use here are from obscure origins too.

Another example of local records showing a different interpretation from official dictionaries occurs in the name of a couple of cottages belonging to the Babworth Hall Estate known as The Biggins. Officially this could be interpreted as coming from the Old English word for building. However, the Estate Diary tells us that Beguines were lay nuns in medieval times and they had a house on this spot. It is to these Beguines that the cottages owe their name. Certainly a long ecclesiastic presence in the parish makes this a possibility.

This section of the Old North Road runs through the archetypal green countryside so beloved of the Georgian poets and calendar artists. Wherever one looks one sees:

'Only thin smoke without flame
From heaps of couch grass
Yet this will go onward the same
Though Dynasties pass.'

The names of the fields are as green as Sherwood Forest, traces of which still straggle from the main forest visible on the horizon.

The Pingle and The Paddock are small grass enclosures gained from the forest, while The Carr was reclaimed from the bog. These names indicate enclosures earlier than the eighteenth century common land enclosures.

The Glebe and Tithe Close are from the time when clergy held their own land, such as that kept by the parson's brother in 'The Canterbury Tales.'

Seed Warrens is a field name that tells of its early function and purpose. 'Seed' indicates that it was set aside to provide grass. 'Warrens' shows that the grass was for breeding rabbits. Furthermore, John Field, in his 'Dictionary of Field Names,' states that where 'seed' was part of a compound name the ground it referred to was always elevated. That is so in the case of Seed Warrens.

In fact, Seed Warrens lies on a ridge that the Danish and Saxon armies fought over and where the coaches rumbled before there were tar-macadam roads. Now from this same ridge, smoke from the power stations along the line of the River Trent twenty miles away, is visible by day. At night the aerial navigation warning lights show up clearly.

The neighbour of Seed Warrens, twenty one and a half acres called Narrow Lands, is a throw back to the medieval system of cultivation by strips. When the grass is at its greenest, especially after winter rain, it is difficult to imagine the generations of feet that have worked this field or trudged over it in peace and in war.

These ancient fields form a lonely landscape especially in the dying light of a winter dusk. Working them day after day, for a lifetime, is a solitary occupation. Hints of loneliness come in the names of farms and fields, such as Botany Bay, found at the remote edge of the parish. The wry name, with its connotations of Australia, separation and a lifetime's absence as a punishment, reflects the feelings of someone who lived here.

Ancient traditions, too, are celebrated in field names. The Rogation Sunday custom of beating the bounds is remembered in fields where the procession halted for particular parts of the ceremony. Thus Gospel Field and Epistle Field survive and, in one part, near the Old North Road is Amen Corner.

With the coming of the railways in the early nineteenth century it was necessary to build a footbridge where there was an existing right of way. The nine and a half acres where such a bridge was built is still called the Forty Steps, even though there are forty four steps over the line.

The fact that this short section of Old North Road is crossed not only by a main rail line but crosses both a river and a canal is reflected in the number of old names connected with water.

Lock Close and New Wharfe Close are self explanatory. Holme Field continues the old English name for a water meadow. Guns Beck Close is one of those compound names where beck implies the existence of a stream.

The Seven Acre Flasher, North Flasher and South Flasher also show that these fields contained a stream as long ago as when Chaucer was writing. They carry on the Middle English name, flasshe, for a stream. As well as these names associated with water there are fields called Pond Piece and Spotted Piece containing dew ponds.

The river, the canal, so many springs, ponds, drains and wells make this dangerous terrain. Old registers and school log books record how many lives were lost through drowning in this parish.

Two fields that were known to have been reclaimed from marshy land at either side of the river bear the strange name of Goachims East and Goachims West. Tradition says these names are connected with water although attempts to trace their origin have been unsuccessful. There is the possibility that the name is a corruption of the Biblical Joachim, the father of the Virgin Mary.

Land was not only reclaimed from marsh and bog but also from the forest. Hirst, the Old English name for copse, occurs in several fields adjacent to the Old North Road. Long Hirst

East, Long Hirst Middle and other fields bearing this name suggest that they were lands reclaimed from the forest earlier than enclosed fields that had a copse planted on them.

The word, hirst, also indicates that between the acres of water meadows and marshes there were patches of dry, barren soil defined in such names as Bracken Ley and Whinney Moor. In fact, the whin, or gorse, still blooms bright and abundant in the hedgerows beside the Old North Road.

The names of some fields have the same charm as that of the words for wild flowers growing in them. Old country names familiar to Chaucer and Shakespeare, they are now mainly found in Middle English glossaries. For instance there is Ladybridge Spinney, where a spinney, or copse, had been planted near to a bridge dedicated to the Virgin Mary. Such a dedication followed the presence of a shrine in the same place during Anglo-Saxon times. Briary Moor received its name from being 'quite over-canopied with . . . eglantine' — or wild rose.

Middle North Ings is an extremely ancient name for pasture land, coming from the Old Norse. Another from the same root is Breck as in East Breck, from the Old Norse 'brekka.'

Upper Neckley is a long, narrow field, similar to a neck, deriving from Old English. In contrast a pointed field is called Picket Close, from a French word that entered the language after the Conquest.

Sometimes field names tell of a kind of agriculture that used to be pursued but is now abandoned. Old Hopyard is such a name. Hops were grown here for a century until 1870 when they failed to compete economically with Kent crops. Nearby, nine acres of ash planted about 1800 for hop poles, still retains its name of Ash Holt, even though it has outlived its function by more than a century.

Gale Carr, at the side of the Old North Road, is not named after the weather but is from the old word for bog myrtle which is gale.

Rape Breck is an unsurprising name nowadays but the kind of rape referred to in the field name is a much older crop used for fodder.

The field called Forest End is still bounded by a strip of woodland from the ancient Forest of Sherwood, a reminder of the proximity of Edwinstowe, the village where King Edwin was killed and where the Major Oak still stands.

Danes Close, beside the river and adjacent to Broom Wood, is an additional reminder of the battle fought here between the Danes and Saxons; it is a name that has outlived its time by well over a thousand years.

The presence of early invaders and even earlier tribes that used the Old North Road before the Romans came is commemorated in part of the road which takes the name, Green Mile. As David Hey says in 'The Making of South Yorkshire,' the inclusion of the word, Green, in the name of the road implies that it was a prehistoric track. The name is repeated in Green Mile Farm and Green Mile Close that stand along this stretch of the Old North Road. Aerial photography has corroborated a prehistoric presence here.

One of the fields records a tragedy. Called Tom Brown's Corner, it was eight acres of grass near where a stream ran into a canal. In a cowshed beside the drain, a farm labourer, Tom Brown, hanged himself about 1830. Nothing now remains of his story except his name, labelling a corner field and preserving his memory.

Shop Close seems an extraordinary name for a field in such a rural position: centuries after it was so called there is no building in sight. The name harks back to a way of life when men first rode horses along the Old North Road, for it was a blacksmith's shop. It fell into disuse when the road was bypassed yet it must have stood here for years providing an essential service for riders and drivers travelling this road. After the road was diverted through Retford the blacksmith's shop became a cowshed but the field retained its original name.

An even more ancient name belongs to a field on Morton Grange land where monks settled with their Rufford Abbey sheep. It is called Chapel Field. On the ground there is no sign of their chapel now, the only remembrance of it comes 'when the ripe and bearded barley is hanging down its head.' At that season the earth gives up its shadows of former ages. The chapel, the house and a lost medieval village that lines this section of road are then visible from the air. Yet, apart from recent aerial photographs, the only memory is in such names as Chapel Field.

Kept alive orally by generations of farmers and workers, these names survive longer than the most ancient of historic houses. They are the same mixture of hard fact and intriguing romance that perpetuates history and man's fascination with it. Like the houses, field names give the receding past 'a local habitation and a name.'

BIBLIOGRAPHY

Professor Arber   *The Story of the Pilgrim Fathers (1897)*

W. Bradford   *Of Plimoth Plantation (ed. 1912)*

C. David Edgar   *Aspects of Nottinghamshire Agricultural History (1950)*

J. Field   *Field Names (1989)*

Firth   *Highways and Byways in Nottinghamshire (1916)*

J. E. B. Gover   *Place Names of Nottinghamshire (1940)*

G. Grigson   *Country Writings (1984)*

Rev. E Jessup   *The Mayflower Story (1962)*
                 Schooldays in Babworth with Ranby (1970)

Johnston   *Place Names of England and Wales (1915)*

Kaye   *A History of Nottinghamshire (1987)*

Arthur Mee   *Nottinghamshire (1938)*

Pevsner   *Buildings of England (1979)*

Plumb   *England in the eighteenth century (1950)*

Repton   *The Red Book (1790)*

Thorold   *Nottinghamshire (Shell Guide 1984)*

Thoroton Society   *Notes on Clergy (1961)*

West   *Sparrows of the Spirit (c. 1950)*

Sir A. Whitaker   *Estate Diary (1898-1929)*

Professor Winks   *An American's Guide to Britain (1977)*

Other Nottinghamshire Books-
by and from John Merrill

WALK GUIDES -
SHORT CIRCULAR WALKS IN THE DUKERIES....0 907496 29 6 ....£7.95
SHORT CIRCULAR WALKS IN SOUTH NOTTINGHAMSHIRE ..0 907496 58 X £6.95
LONG CIRCULAR WALKS IN NOTTINGHAMSHIRE ....1 874754 22 5 ....£6.95
THE LITTLE JOHN CHALLENGE WALK ....0 907496 46 6 ....£4.95
DERBYSHIRE & NOTTINGHAMSHIRE CANAL WALKS .... 0 907496 30 X £12.95
SHORT CIRCULAR WALKS ON THE GRANTHAM CANAL .....9781903627563 ....£10.95
SHORT CIRCULAR WALKS ON THE CHESTERFIELD CANAL ....1-903627-43-5.....................£10.95

NOTTINGHAMSHIRE HERITAGE SERIES -
THE OLD NORTH ROAD by Joan Board ....ISBN 0 946404-62-3................£6.50
PILGRIM COUNTRY - A TO Z by Joan Board ....ISBN 1 -84173-002-5 ....£9.95
THE GREAT NORTH ROAD THROUGH NOTTINGHAMSHIRE by Joan Board
ISBN 978-0-9553691-5-5...£10.95.
BASFORD - VILLAGE TO SUBURB by A.S.Bowley ....ISBN 1-903627-75-3.........£7.50
WOLLATON HALL by Elizabeth May ....ISBN 0 946404 02 5......£7.95
BELL TALES by Ztan Zmith .....978-0-946404-43-8 ....£5.95
SOME NOTTINGHAMSHIRE INN AND PUB STORIES by Ztan Zmith 1-874754-99-3........... £6.95
WHAT A LIFE & other Nottinghamshire Tales by Ztan Smith ....978-0-9553691-9-3 ....£6.95
NAN SCOTT- The face at the Window by Ztan Zmith .....0-946404-33-x £5.95
THE VILLAGE OF ELKESLEY - a comprehensive history - by Alan Hirst. 9780955651151....£12.95

GHOST & LEGENDS SERIES -
GHOST HUNTING AROUND NOTTINGHAMSHIRE by R. Robb ..ISBN 0 94640....................£7.50
GHOSTS & LEGENDS OF NEWARK by Rosemary Robb.....ISBN 0 946404.....................£6.50
THE RESTLESS SPIRIT - more ghost stories from the East Midlands by R Robb £7.50
WARTIME GHOST STORIES AND MYTHS - Vol. 1 by R Robb...ISBN 1-903627 ....£7.50
A GHOSTLY GUIDE TO NOTTINGHAMSHIRE by C. Staton..1-903627-48-6.......................£6.95
RHYME AND REASON...Some Nottinghamshire Folk Tales by Ztan Zmith.. 9781841730035.....£6.95

Full list from -
THE JOHN MERRILL FOUNDATION.
32, Holmesdale, Waltham Cross, Hertfordshire EN8 8QY

Tel/Fax - 01992 762776
email - marathonhiker@aol.com   www.johnmerrillwalkguides.co.uk